Contents

Introduction	6
Evolution	8
Cetacean Family	10
Adaptations	12
Whale Senses	14
Communication	16
Diving and Displays	18
Social Ties	20
Whale Habits	22
Rorqual Whales	24
Blue Whales	26
Slow-Swimming Baleen Whales	28
Toothed Whales	30
Killer Whales	32
Dolphins	34
The World of Dolphins	36
River Dolphins	38
Porpoises	40
Whaling and Conservation	42
Glossary	44
Answers	46
Introduction	48
Marine Habitats	50
What is For Dinner?	52

Marine Biology	54
Sponges and Anemones	56
Snails, Clams and Oysters	58
Sea Stars	60
Jellyfish	62
Crustaceans	64
Eels	66
Whales	68
Dolphins and Porpoises	70
Dugongs and Manatees	72
Pinnipeds	74
Monsters of the sea	76
Marine Reptiles	78
Coral Reefs	80
Octopus and Squid	82
Extinct Sea Creatures	84
Glossary	86
Answers	88

WHALES AND DOLPHINS

Introduction

Some of the largest living creatures on Earth, whales and dolphins have attracted a lot of human interest. These sea animals are not fish and are more closely related to mammals. They are warm-blooded animals that breathe with their lungs. They swim to the surface of the water to breathe.

These fascinating animals are found in oceans all over the world. Whales, dolphins and porpoises belong to the family of cetaceans, which are a kind of marine mammal. They are large, intelligent and aquatic animals. These animals are widely hunted for their skin, oil and meat.

Evolution

Cetaceans are direct descendants of terrestrial mammals, such as pigs, hippos, camels, etc. The vast resources of food in oceans attracted these early mammals, which eventually evolved into marine mammals. These animals gradually moved from land to sea in various stages.

Which is the oldest known cetacean?

Facts
- The bones inside the front flippers of whales and dolphins have an arrangement similar to those of the human hand.
- Squalodontids are believed to be the first whales that could produce sounds.

Mesonychids

The earliest ancestors of whales were known as mesonychids. They were hoofed animals with triangular teeth that lived primarily on land. Mesonychids were essentially carnivorous and used to hunt for food in freshwater habitats. Pakicetus, the oldest known cetacean, was found in the river deposits in Pakistan.

Protocetids

Protocetids evolved around 45 million years ago. These animals developed many characteristics similar to modern-day whales, such as flukes and the ability to hear underwater. The nostrils were pushed back and evolved into blowholes.

Ambulocetus and remingtonocetids

Ambulocetus marked the next stage in the development of cetaceans. These amphibious mammals were approximately the size of a sea lion. Their feet were better adapted for swimming in water. They hunted like crocodiles by catching prey in shallow waters. Remingtonocetids were another kind of mammals that were better adapted to underwater life. They were more like sea otters that swam by undulating their spine.

Basilosaurids and dorudontids

Basilosaurids and dorudontids were fully marine cetaceans that largely resembled modern whales and lived their entire lives in oceans. Basilosaurids were large in size, growing up to 18 m long, while dorudontids were almost the size of dolphins. These animals retained their useless hind feet and had a small brain. They lacked the melon (a fat-filled organ inside the head) found in their predecessors that is used to make sounds. They finally evolved into the two main groups of the modern-day cetaceans—odontocetes and mysticetes.

Cetacean Family

Whales, dolphins and porpoises belong to the family of cetaceans. The term 'whale' is often used to describe all cetaceans. These mammals have a hairless body, reduced hind limbs and flippers. The whale family can de divided into baleen whales and toothed whales.

Toothed whales

Toothed whales are a diverse group. These whales have peg-like teeth that are designed for catching and gripping their prey. They are primarily hunters and feed on squid, fish, crabs and starfish. They have a single blowhole. Beaked whales, narwhals, beluga whales, sperm whales, dolphins and porpoises belong to the family of toothed whales.

Baleen whales

Baleen whales are also known as filter-feeding whales because of the whalebone or baleen curtains. These whales have thin broom-like bristles in their mouth instead of teeth. This fibrous mat falls like a curtain from their upper jaw. The baleen plates help these whales to filter food from water. Baleen whales are usually larger than toothed whales and have two blowholes rather than one. Grey whales, rorqual whales and right whales belong to the family of baleen whales.

Dolphins and porpoises

Dolphins and porpoises are toothed whales. However, they are the smaller members of the whale family. Dolphins have a distinct beak and conical teeth. They form the largest group of cetaceans. Porpoises are generally smaller than dolphins and have spade-like teeth. Unlike dolphins that have a melon-shaped forehead, porpoises generally have a blunt forehead.

The grey whale belongs to the family of _____.

Facts

- Toothed whales are considered as one of the most intelligent animals on Earth.
- Baleen, or whalebone, was once used to make combs and corsets and even parasols for women.

Adaptations

Cetaceans may look like fish and eat like them, but they are warm-blooded mammals. They are known as highly specialized due to their numerous adaptations.

Respiration

Whales breathe through their lungs just like mammals. Instead of nostrils, they have blowholes that are located at the top of their body. This allows them to remain submerged while breathing with only their head exposed at the surface. As whales come to the surface to breathe, they exhale and release nitrogen, water and mucus in a blast. This discharge often looks like a spout and is followed by quick inhaling. A thick membrane shuts the blowhole while in water.

Locomotion

Whales and dolphins have a streamlined body that is adapted to swimming. Their hind limbs are modified in the form of flippers that are used as paddles for stopping or turning. Their tail has flukes that help propel them in a vertical motion as opposed to the horizontal motion of fish. Some whales also have a dorsal fin located at the top of their body that helps them to take sudden turns.

Warm-blooded

Whales are warm-blooded mammals, and their core body temperature remains the same. Hence, it is important for them to maintain their body temperature in the cold waters of the ocean. Whales and dolphins have a thick layer of blubber located right beneath their skin that prevents the loss of heat from the body. Their high-density blubber is made of fats and fibrous tissues and can be as thick as 50 cm. The circulatory system of whales is also specially adapted to keep their body warm in diverse environments.

Facts

- A blue whale can produce up to 50 tonnes of blubber.
- A whale's four-chambered heart and large arteries allow blood to quickly pass through its body and reach the vital organs effectively.

Whales and dolphins breathe through gills. (True/False)

Whale Senses

Whales have the same senses as other mammals. However, their senses have adapted themselves completely to the marine environment they inhabit. Cetaceans do not have any sense of smell. There are mixed opinions as to whether they have the sense of taste, but some dolphins have been noted to show sensitivity to taste and can even taste water to know about the available preys.

Eyesight

Whales hunt for their food in the deep seas and oceans where little or no sunlight reaches. Their eyes are well-adapted to see in low-intensity light. They can see up to a distance of 10.7 m in water.

Facts

- Whales do not have tear ducts in their eyes. Instead, they have oil ducts that secrete an oily substance to keep their eyes clean.
- A whale's ears are adapted to hearing only under the water and not in the air.

Which technique do whales and dolphins use to perceive their environment?

Sound

Whales and dolphins have an excellent hearing power in water. They do not have any outer ears or flaps. While baleen whales hear through their outer ear canal, toothed whales hear through the fat pad in their jaw, which transmits the sound to their middle ear. This middle ear is filled with fluid and foam. Whales are able to perceive their environment by using echolocation—the technique of sound reflection.

Magnetic sense

Scientists argue that whales may have a magnetic sense based on small magnetite crystals found in certain cells of their body. They use it to sense Earth's magnetic field, which helps them in navigation. Sperm whales are known to migrate great distances with the help of their magnetic sense.

Touch

The sense of touch is very important to whales. They have a very thin skin that is rich in blood vessels and nerves. They are known to rub and caress their partners during the time they are breeding. Physical touch provides comfort and warmth to the calves. Most cetaceans also have tactile whiskers on their snout.

Communication

Cetaceans are believed to be very noisy animals that produce some of the loudest sounds. They use sound for orientation, hunting, communication and navigation in deep waters. Baleen whales are known to produce low-frequency sounds that can travel hundreds of kilometres in water.

Echolocation

Whales produce sounds under water that bounce back and return to them in the form of echoes. These echoes enable them to determine the shape, size, speed and direction of the surrounding objects. Toothed whales produce clicking sounds that help them to receive and interpret the resulting echoes.

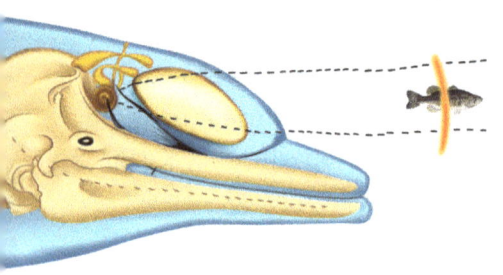

Facts

- Whales of a particular area are known to sing similar songs that are probably learnt by repetition, whereas whales in different regions sing entirely different songs.
- The communication between whales through sounds is hampered by the noise caused in the oceans by ships, submarines and marine seismic surveys.

Body language

Whales often communicate through various gestures and body movements. A forceful spout may indicate aggression, whereas the slapping of flippers may indicate excitement, arousal or aggression.

> Which whale is known to sing songs?

Sounds

Whales communicate with each other through low-frequency grunts, thumps and moans. Most toothed whales produce a series of high-frequency clicks and whistles in rapid succession. These sounds are produced within a cavity in their head and comes out of the blowhole. The melon in toothed whales helps to focus the series of sound waves produced by them.

Songs

Baleen whales such as the humpback whales are known to sing melodious songs that are usually mating calls to their partners. Whale songs may last for 30 minutes and are often divided into different themes. Baleen whales often make calls as a greeting, for assembly or for threat identification.

Diving and Displays

Whales are powerful animals that rule the waters they live in. They are deep divers and display a wide variety of acrobatics at the ocean's surface. Dolphins have entertained humans all over the world by their playful nature.

Diving

Most whales and dolphins live near the surface of water, but many of them dive deep into the ocean in search of food. They have special adaptations that enable them to withstand high-pressure diving. Whales often slow their heartbeat, and their blood supplies oxygen only to their vital organs, such as the brain, heart, etc. Most dolphins and whales breathe every 15 minutes, but can hold their breath for long durations while diving. Sperm whales are diving champions and can hold their breath for as long as 2 hours during a deep-water plunge.

Lobtailing

Whales often jump out of water and slap their tail or flukes on the surface of water. Known as lobtailing, this activity creates a huge splash and is repeated a number of times in an instance. Lobtailing is usually associated with power displays or aggression.

> The action of whales raising their body vertically out of water is called _____.

Breaching

Whales often display a majestic feat of leaping out of water and slapping the ocean's surface with their huge body. A leap where a whale exposes only 40 per cent of its body is known as a lunge. Whales swim at high speeds to get out of water and may sometimes turn around while breaching. Breaching is done for playful purposes or to get rid of parasites.

Spy-hopping

Whales often raise their body vertically out of water and turn around to take a look. This activity is known as spy-hopping. While doing this, they hold their body out of water for a considerable period of time by kicking their tails. Whales also spy-hop to look for preys.

Facts

- Whales are often seen resting at the ocean's surface with their back, head or dorsal fin outside water and their tail trailing down. This activity is known as logging.
- Whales roll themselves a complete 360 degrees to prepare for a surprise attack.

Social Ties

Whales and dolphins have great social ties and are usually found in groups that are known as pods. Pods are usually formed on the basis of age and sex. Since whales can live for many years, they develop deep bonds with the members of their group. The members of a pod travel and hunt together.

Dominant bulls and midwives

There are more females in a pod than males. Males usually aid in hunting and ensure that everyone in the group gets food. A single male is often considered as the dominant bull of the pod and undertakes the responsibility of protecting its cows (female whales) and calves from predators. Midwives are female members that assist a pregnant cow in delivering and caring for the baby. A baby whale needs to be brought to the surface of water immediately after its birth for fresh air. The midwives not only help the mothers in doing this but also babysit the calves in their mother's absence or death.

Mating competition

During the breeding season, bachelor males try to woo the females by singing or displaying fighting performances. The females decide which males they want to be with depending on their strength and stamina. A couple goes through a brief courtship period before mating. A female may mate with many males during the breeding period.

Cow and the calf

The strongest bond among the whale family is that of the cows and the calves. A whale gives birth after a gestation period of 9–18 months. The calf stays close to its mother, often maintaining physical contact for warmth and support. The mother deeply cares for its young one and nourishes the baby with its own milk.

What are baby whales called?

Facts

- Whales are known to show signs of mourning if a member of the group dies.
- Female whales can become very aggressive while protecting their young ones.

Whale Habits

Cetaceans are one of the most intelligent group of animals on Earth. Their capacity to communicate and understand each other is considered unique among mammals. They display various interesting habits and behaviours, the meaning of some still being unclear.

No sleep!

Whales and dolphins have to frequently come to the surface of water to breathe. They have to remain partially conscious even in their sleep for fear of drowning. They never go into deep sleep because one hemisphere of their brain is active even during sleep. Some researches show that whales and dolphins don't sleep after birth. For about a month, the newborns and their mothers stay continuously active. With time, they start following the sleeping patterns of adult whales.

Drinking water

Cetaceans cannot drink seawater just like us. They fulfil all their water requirements from the fish they eat. They may chose to eat different kinds of fish depending on the amount of water or calories they need. Cetaceans have efficient kidneys that are used to filter out excess salt from the body.

Migration

Whales migrate long distances each year. They move from cold water areas to warmer regions for breeding and calving purposes. The developments in radio and satellite technology have made it possible to track and understand the migratory routes of whales. Humpback whales are known to migrate up to a distance of 25,000 km each year.

Facts

- Beluga whales are capable of showing facial expressions.
- A study says that sperm whales might have their own individual names.

Which whale is capable of showing facial expressions?

Rorqual Whales

Rorqual whales are the family of the largest whales that include humpback whales, minke whales, blue whales, Bryde's whales, Omura's whales and sei whales. These whales are slender and have a short, pointed dorsal fin. These fast-swimming whales usually have a dark body and a pale underside.

Great gulpers

Rorqual whales are characterized by thin and long grooves or pleats in their skin that run down their throat. These skin pleats expand like a balloon when these whales feed. These whales feed in a unique manner that is known as lunge feeding. They dive to great depths of the ocean and lunge towards a swarm or group of fish and krill with their mouth open wide. Once they gulp down large amounts of prey, they push out water by contracting their throats. The food is caught in the thick baleen plates on their upper jaw, which is then swallowed whole.

Which is the smallest rorqual whale?

Fin whales

Fin whales are next in size to blue whales. These fastest-moving whales are distinguished by an asymmetrical colouring of their face. Their left lip and baleen plates are a dark shade, while their right lip and jaw are white. This is probably due to the fact that they feed in a tilted position.

Humpback whales

Humpback whales are spectacular animals characterized by small bumps on their head and extremely long flippers that are usually one-third of their body length. They are known for the melodious and complicated series of songs produced by the males during breeding. They are true acrobats and display their energetic nature by slapping their flippers and tails. During a five-month long migration, humpbacks do not eat anything and depend on their fat reserves for survival.

Facts

- Minke whales are the smallest type of rorqual whales and can be often seen breaching using water currents.
- Fin whales use their powerful flukes as a weapon against sharks and hunting boats.

Blue Whales

Blue whales belong to the family of baleen whales and are the largest living creatures on Earth. They also hold the record for being the loudest animals. They are found in all the oceans of the world and travel as far as the tropics in winters and the polar regions in summers.

Size

The gigantic blue whale can grow up to 30m long—as big as a nine-storey building. They can weigh up to 200 tonnes, and their tongue alone can weigh as much as an elephant. A blue whale's heart is almost as big as a small automobile and its largest arteries are big enough for people to swim in it. Its blowhole shoots up to 9 m.

Diet

Interestingly, the largest animal on Earth eats the tiny krill—an animal that is one-thousandth of its own size. A single blue whale can eat up to 4–8 tonnes of krill in a day. Baby blue whales are the largest babies on our planet. Due to the rich and nutritious milk of their mother, they can gain up to 4.5 kg of weight every hour.

Solitary whales

Blue whales are the loners of the whale family. They are usually seen traversing the oceans alone or in pairs. A group of blue whales may get together in regions with abundant food supply. These massive whales have been hunted down by humans for their baleen and blubber, and are now facing the grave threat of extinction.

Which is the largest living creature on Earth?

Facts

- A single breath of a blue whale has enough air to fill nearly 2,000 balloons.
- A blue whale's nostril is big enough for a toddler to crawl in.

Slow-Swimming Baleen Whales

Right whales, bowhead whales and grey whales belong to the family of baleen whales. Unlike rorquals, these whales are slow swimmers and do not have skin grooves that can inflate while feeding. They mainly feed on zooplankton and small fish.

Right whales

Right whales are the rarest of all large whales. They are characterized by a rotund body and a massive head. Whale hunters identified them as the 'right whales' to hunt since they are slow swimmers and have large amounts of blubber that keep them afloat after they are killed. They were nearly hunted to extinction for their valuable oil and baleen. Right whales have huge concrete-like growths on their head that are known as callosities. These hardened patches of skin usually appear white due to the growth of whale lice on them. Right whales are divided into the northern right whales and the southern right whales that stay in their respective hemispheres and do not venture away from the equator.

The callosities of right whales appear white due to the presence of _____.

Grey whales

Grey whales have a mottled appearance and are characterized by a dorsal hump on their body. They are the most parasitized of all whales. Their dark skin has many patches and growths of barnacles and whale lice. These whales also feed from the ocean floor by scooping up their prey along with mud and sediments. They are known to make the longest migration by any animal and usually travel near the shores.

Bowhead whales

Bowhead whales are known for their enormous bow-shaped skulls. They are the longest baleen whales in the whale community. These whales spend their entire life in the Arctic and use their massive body and beak-like upper jaw to break the ice and breathe from the surface of the ocean. They are usually black in colour with a white chin that is lined by black spots. Bowhead whales have a thick blubber that helps them to survive in their cold habitat.

Facts

- The pygmy right whale is the smallest of all baleen whales.
- Recent studies have shown that bowhead whales may live up to 200 years.

Toothed Whales

Toothed whales are usually smaller than baleen whales and have few or several teeth lined in their jaws. These whales include sperm whales, beluga whales, pilot whales, narwhals, etc.

Sperm whales

The largest toothed animals, sperm whales, have a large, squared head accounting for almost one-third of their weight. A sperm whale may have 18 or 26 pairs of conical teeth on its lower jaw. They are named after a waxy substance produced in their head that is known as spermaceti. This fluid is used to give them extra buoyancy while diving.

Facts

- Belugas are known as 'sea canaries' because of their songs and chatter, which can be heard well above the ocean's surface.
- The Inuits hunt the narwhals for their long tusks and skin—an important source of Vitamin C.

Beluga whales

Beluga whales are white-coloured Arctic dwellers. They are known for their distinctive vocalizations and rounded forehead. A bulbous melon inside their head that often changes shape is used for sound production. They have a very flexible neck that allows them to nod and move their head all around. These finless whales are hunted largely by the orcas and polar bears when they get covered by ice during winters. They are usually born grey but moult as they grow and become white in colour.

Narwhals

Narwhals are also known as the unicorns of the sea because of a unique sword-like protrusion from their upper jaws. They have only two teeth in their upper jaw, may grow as a tusk in the case of some males. These unique horns are used to spear food or to dig the ocean mud. They have sensory tissues that can sense the salinity of water as well as the change in temperature. They travel in groups and usually feed on squid, mollusks, fish and crustaceans. Males often engage in tusk fights to attract a female.

> Which whales are called sea canaries?

Killer Whales

Orcas or killer whales are the biggest members of the dolphin family and are found in all the oceans of the world. These toothed whales are also known as the 'wolves of the sea' due to their hunting capabilities. They were initially called 'whale killers' because of their ferocious attacks on other whales, including baby blue whales.

Feeding and hunting

Orcas are top predators that feed on a diverse variety of sea creatures. They eat anything from fish, squids, birds and penguins to sea lions and other whales. They use a series of high-pitched clicks to stun their prey. Their upper and lower jaws consist of 45–60 conical teeth, which interlock together and allow them to get a strong grip on their prey. Orcas are known to hunt in a team by using a well-defined strategy. They often work together and attack a school of fish by encircling them. Some orcas slide on to a beach and scare away penguins or seals into the sea where the other whales are waiting to attack them. While hunting a baby whale, they chase and encircle it, not allowing it to go up to the surface to breathe and it eventually dies from drowning.

Speed masters

Orcas are black in colour with patches of white on their underside. With a stout and tapered body, they are also the fastest swimmers of the whale world and can swim at a speed of **48 kmph**.

Social life

Orcas are highly social animals and live in closely-knit groups known as pods. These pods are led by females. The leaders are very protective of the members of the pod and share the responsibility of caring for the young, the sick and the injured.

What is the other name for killer whales?

Facts

- Different orca pods have different dialects and means of communication.
- Humans are considered as the only true enemies of orcas.

Dolphins

The family of dolphins consists of almost 40 species. Dolphins are among the most intelligent animals and have always fascinated humans with their playful and friendly nature. They are easily recognized by a distinctive beak and a sloping forehead due to the presence of melon inside their head.

Intelligence

Dolphins are the closest marine friends of humans. In captivity, they are considered to be capable of learning things and also understanding simple commands such as 'hold the ball'. Dolphins have been known to use tools. Some species are known to gather sponge at the end of their beak. This act protects them against injury while foraging for food at the ocean bed. They are also known to recognize themselves in a mirror.

What is the activity in which dolphins hit fish and throw them out of water called?

Hunting and feeding

Dolphins usually feed on fish and squid. They often hunt in large groups by encircling and herding a school of fish into tight balls known as bait balls. Strand feeding is a method in which dolphins attack a school of fish and drive them out of water on rocky reefs. They consume the fish that have been washed out on the beach. Dolphins often hit small fish with their powerful flukes and throw them out of water. This activity is known as fish whacking.

Bow diving

Dolphins are also known to travel and surf waves alongside boats and ships. This playful activity at the bow of the boats is known as bow diving. In this manner, dolphins are believed to conserve energy by riding on ocean currents. Their aerial acrobatics, such as flipping and spinning, amaze spectators both in marine parks as well as the wild.

Facts

- Dolphins have the ability to recover from extreme wounds and injuries such as shark bite.
- In the US, the military trains bottlenose dolphins to locate sea mines and enemy divers.

The World of Dolphins

Dolphins belong to the family of toothed whales. They are mostly carnivorous and feed on a wide variety of fish, squid and crustaceans. They are usually grey in colour with darker backs. The teeming family of dolphins include killer whales, pilot whales, common dolphins and spinner dolphins.

Common dolphins

Common dolphins have the most complex colour pattern of all cetaceans. The varied colours on their body are formed almost like an hourglass. They are medium-sized dolphins, and the males are usually longer and heavier than females. Common dolphins are found in warm tropical waters.

Spinner dolphins

The spinner dolphin is a species of dolphins that can leap out of water up to a height of 3.5 m—they often spin three to four times in the air before splashing back into the water. Their unusual swimming is a way of communicating. These dolphins are known to swim with tuna fish and are often victims of the tuna fishery industry. They get entangled in fishing nets along with tunas.

Bottlenose dolphins

Bottlenose dolphins are the most common and well-known species of dolphins. These dolphins have a curved jaw that appears as if they are smiling. They can have as many as 88–100 teeth in their jaws. They are called 'bottlenose' due to their elongated rostrum. These dolphins are famous for their interaction with and friendliness towards humans. They are known to rescue injured divers by raising them above the water. They are also known to protect divers from shark attacks.

Risso's dolphins

Risso's dolphins are usually grey in colour with a distinct white scarring on their body. This scarring is either a result of dolphin and squid bites or due to parasites. These dolphins do not have any teeth in their upper jaw.

Facts

- Dolphins can jump up to 7 m above water.
- Every dolphin has a unique whistle, much like the varied thumbprints of humans. They identify each other by these whistles.

How far can a dolphin jump out of water?

River Dolphins

Although all cetaceans are marine mammals and are found in oceans and seas, some dolphins are also found in freshwater habitats. The Amazon River, the Indus River, the Ganges and the Yangtze River are home to some fascinating species of dolphins. River dolphins use echolocation to find their way around in muddy waters.

Botos

Botos or the Amazon River dolphins are the largest of all river dolphins. They have very long beaks and sharp, strong teeth that allow them to prey on fish, crustaceans and even turtles. Botos come in beautiful shades of pink. They can move their neck up to 180 degrees, allowing them to hunt efficiently at river bottoms.

Indus River dolphins

The Indus River dolphins found in certain regions of Pakistan are an endangered species of mammals. These dolphins are blind, and their eyes can differentiate only between light and dark. They emit sounds that hit objects, bounce back and are received as echoes. Because of poor eyesight, they depend on the sensitive tentacles on their flippers to feel the river bottom. Hence, they are often seen swimming sideways. Their thin and long beaks help them to forage for food on riverbeds.

Yangtze River dolphins

The Chinese River dolphin also known as 'baiji' lived in the Yangtze River. This magnificent species of dolphin was declared extinct in 2007. Increased industrialization and the pollution caused by it in the Yangtze River destroyed the natural habitat of these mammals. The construction of the Three Gorges Dam on the river and high shipping traffic made it impossible for these blind dolphins to survive.

What is the other name for the Amazon River dolphin?

Facts

- Unlike ocean dolphins, river dolphins have finger-like grooves on their flippers. Their snout is around four times longer than that of ocean dolphins.
- The Amazon River dolphins are known to swim upside down.

Porpoises

Porpoises are smaller members of the cetacean family. They have a stout body, a small rounded head and no beak. Porpoises have been divided into six species. They have a very well-developed air sinus system in their head. They feed primarily on fish and shellfish.

Finless porpoises

Finless porpoises are mainly found in the coastal waters of Asia. A freshwater variety of finless porpoises is also found in the Yangtze River in China. As the name suggests, finless porpoises do not have any dorsal fins. Instead, they have a rough denticulated area on their back, which is used to carry calves as they cling to their mother's back.

What do porpoises eat?

Dall's porpoises

Dall's porpoises have a unique body shape with a thick stout body and a small head. They are fast and strong swimmers and are also considered as one of the most evolved cetaceans. These porpoises are found along the Pacific Coast from Alaska to Southern California. Unlike other porpoises, Dall's porpoises are very active and are often seen bow riding near boats.

Harbour porpoises

Harbour porpoises are shy and elusive and mainly inhabit harbours, bays or other shallow waters. One of the smallest cetaceans, these porpoises can venture as far as estuaries, rivers and tidal channels. They are capable of diving deep but prefer staying close to the water's surface. Every 25 seconds, they come up to the surface to breathe. They breathe with a deep puffing noise similar to a sneeze.

- Porpoises have a short and mostly immobile neck.
- The meat of harbour porpoises was considered a delicacy during the Middle Ages.

Whaling and Conservation

In the prehistoric times, hunting whales was considered to be a big game or sport. Over time, whaling became a commercial business in America, Russia and some other countries. Whale hunting posed a grave danger to whales since they reproduce only once a year. Most whales produce a single offspring during a pregnancy and twins are rare.

Conservation

In 1946, many countries joined hands to sign an international whaling convention that aimed at saving the dwindling populations of whales. Several restrictions have been imposed on whaling practices. Whaling for commercial purposes has been banned in many countries. Whales and dolphins are also conserved and bred in captivity in various marine parks and natural habitats.

Other threats

Increased sea noise, speeding cargo ships and pollution have disturbed the communication and migratory patterns of whales. Whale strandings on sea shores are becoming very common. To deal with this threat, many regions of the sea that are inhabited by cetaceans are being preserved as travel-free zones.

Blubber and baleen

A single whale yielded large amounts of meat owing to its great size. Gradually, people became interested in the rich oil obtained from the blubber, which was used as a fuel to light up lamps. Whalebone or baleen was highly prized and was used to make ladies' corsets and umbrellas. With the invention of the harpoon gun and swift speed boats, hunting these mammals became much easier.

Baleens were earlier used to make ladies' corsets and _____.

Facts

- Underwater disturbances from ships, military operations and oil and gas operations are some of the threats that should be minimized to protect and conserve sea creatures.
- Despite a moratorium on commercial whaling that came into force in 1986, Japan continues to kill whales.

Glossary

Acrobatic: to balance one's body with great skill while jumping, leaping and turning it

Ancestor: a predecessor or an organism that lived years ago and from which the modern forms have developed

Blubber: a thick layer of body fat

Buoyancy: the ability to float

Calorie: a unit for measuring the energy an organism gets from food

Crustacean: an animal with many legs and a hard shell for protection, such as crabs

Dialect: a form of language that is spoken by a particular group of organisms

Diverse: very different

Elusive: one that is difficult to find or catch

Endangered species: an animal species that is on the verge of dying out

Environment: the natural world, including land, water and air, that determines a living being's form and habitat and affects its survival

Equator: an imaginary line on the earth's surface that divides it into two hemispheres

Extinction: a situation where a species of an organism is dead and no longer exists

Flipper: a wide, flat body part used by whales and some other sea organisms for swimming

Frequency: the number of times something has happened

Gestation period: the time period during which a baby develops inside its mother

Gigantic: very large or huge

Habitat: a place where a particular organism lives

Industrialization: setting up more factories and machines for business development

Mottle: to have spots or patches on the skin

Offspring: a baby

Parasite: an organism that lives on other organisms for food and nutrition

Parasitize: to exploit an organism as a parasite

Pollution: the presence of harmful substances in the atmosphere

Prey: an animal that is hunted by predators or other animals for food

Rotund: round and fat body

Satellite: an object that is sent into space to revolve around Earth in order to receive and send information

Seismic: a vibration of earth

Stout: strong and heavy

Submarine: a vehicle that can travel both underwater and on the surface of water

Tactile: somebody who likes to touch for displaying warmth or care

Taper: to reduce in thickness towards one end

Unicorn: an imaginary horse-like creature that has a long horn on its snout

Moratorium: a temporary ban on an activity

Answers

Page No. 8	Pakicetus
Page No. 11	Baleen whales
Page No. 13	False
Page No. 14	Echolocation
Page No. 16	Humpback whale
Page No. 19	Spy-hopping
Page No. 21	Calves
Page No. 23	Beluga whale
Page No. 24	Minke whale
Page No. 27	Blue whale
Page No. 28	Whale lice
Page No. 31	Beluga whales
Page No. 33	Orcas
Page No. 34	Fish whacking
Page No. 37	About 7 m
Page No. 39	Boto
Page No. 40	Fish and shellfish
Page No. 43	Umbrellas

SEA CREATURES

Introduction

A sea creature refers to an animal that lives in the sea. Sea creatures are of different types and they belong to different families. They vary in size from being very big like the blue whale to very small like zooplankton. Sea creatures can be broadly classified into fishes, mammals, mollusks, shellfish and reptiles. The sea is not made up of only animals. There are a variety of underwater plants as well. Underwater plants are very important for our ecology.

They are useful for animals as well as humans. The major category of deep-sea plants is the phytoplankton. The largest marine forms are called seaweeds. These plants are useful for providing food to sea creatures and humans. Some of the other common sea plants are blue-green coral, feather star, sea fan and giant barrel sponge. All see creatures depend on each other for survival and food. No member can survive independently , whether it is microscopic or gigantic.

Marine Habitats

Marine habitat means an area or environment where an animal or plant lives naturally. In a habitat, several plants and animals depend upon each other for survival. The most important elements in a marine habitat are planktons, nektons and benthos.

Benthos

Benthos is a group of plants and animals that live near the bottom of the sea. They include many small fishes, crustaceans and mollusks. Benthos eat plankton and are in turn eaten up by nektons.

Facts

- Planktons are the starting points of every marine food chain.
- The number of nektons in the sea increases as you go deeper into the sea.

Plankton

Plankton is a collection of floating microscopic animals and plants at the bottom of the sea. Planktons are the major source of food for sea creatures. There are three types of plankton – zooplankton, phytoplankton and bacterioplankton. Phytoplankton are microscopic plants like algae that float on the sea bed. All marine animals eat them. Zooplankton are tiny floating animals eaten by small fishes. Bacterioplankton are tiny bacteria found in large numbers.

Nekton

Nekton is a collection of free-moving animals. Their motion is independent of water and wind motion. There are three types of nektons – Chordates, Mollusks and Arthropods. Chordates include bony, cartilaginous fishes like sharks and several species of reptiles like turtles, snakes and crocodiles. Chordates also include mammals like whales, porpoises and seals. Mollusc nektons include squid and octopus. Arthropod nektons are shrimps, crabs and lobsters. Most nektons feed on zooplankton whereas herbivorous nektons are very rare.

Name a type of nekton

What is For Dinner?

Food chain is the transfer of energy from one species to another. It is a sequence of who eats whom to get nutrition. Within a food chain, some living things produce energy (producers) while others use energy (consumers). Plants are producers because they have to make their own food (photosynthesis). Animals are consumers because they eat plants and other animals for energy.

Elements in a food chain

A food chain starts with the primary source of energy – the sun. The next in the chain are autotrophs or primary producers. Autotrophs like plants make their own food from the primary source. Next in the chain are primary consumers. Primary consumers are herbivores like rabbits. They eat the primary producers. Secondary consumers like snakes eat the primary consumers. Tertiary consumers like owls eat secondary consumers. Tertiary consumers are eaten by quaternary consumers like hawks. These are finally eaten by animals with no natural enemies like alligators and polar bears. Detritivores like vultures eat dead organisms and are broken down by decomposers like bacteria and fungi. All elements are very important. The absence of one can be dangerous for the entire chain.

Facts
- Energy which is transferred from one member of the food chain to another is a form of heat.
- A network of food chains is called a food web.

What are primary producers also called?

Marine food chain

Phytoplankton are the starting point of the marine food chain. They are eaten by zooplankton. Zooplankton are eaten by small fish and crustaceans like crabs and lobsters. Small fish are eaten by big fish like penguins and whales. Big fish are eaten by large mammals like polar mammals.

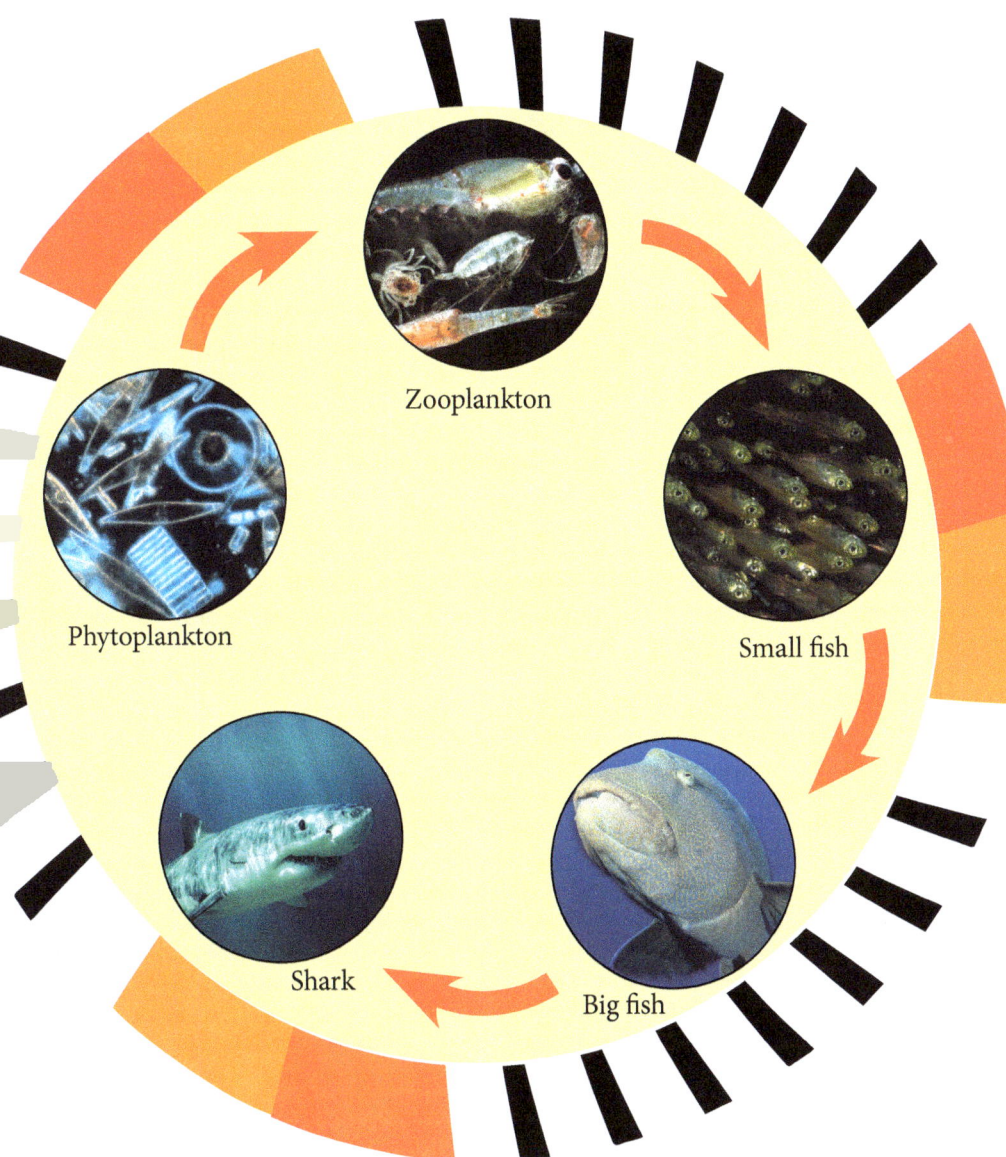

Marine Biology

Marine biology is the scientific study of organisms in water bodies like seas and oceans. Marine life is a vast resource of providing food, medicine and raw materials. Marine organisms contribute significantly to the oxygen cycle and are involved in the regulation of the Earth's climate. All plant and animal life forms are included in the study of marine biology, be it small or large.

Marine Biologists

A marine biologist studies marine biology, meaning life forms of water bodies from a scientific perspective. Many people think that mammals are the only subject of study for marine biologists. Marine biologists study different areas of marine life. Some of the fields which marine biologists are now entering include environmental marine biology, Ichthyology and marine mammalogy.

Environmental marine biology determines the quality of the marine environment to ensure that water quality is sufficient to sustain a healthy environment and is free of sediments or pollutants. Ichthyology studies all aspects of fish from their classification to their evolution and behaviour. Marine mammalogy studies families of mammals in the sea, their behaviour, habitat, health, reproduction and population.

Technology

The oceans are difficult to study, as they are vast and foreign to humans. Different tools used to study the oceans include sampling mechanisms such as bottom trawls and plankton nets. Tracking methods and devices such as photo-identification research, satellite tags, and hydrophones are also used to avoid manual effort as it involves several dangers of sea monsters.

Facts
- 50-80% of all life on Earth is found underwater.
- 99% of the planet's living space is underwater.

What is the study of fish classification called?

Sponges and Anemones

There are three types of mammals: monotremes, marsupials and placental mammals. Placental mammals have a placenta in their body, which helps in the exchange of nutrients and wastes between the Mother's blood and that of the fetus. A well-developed placenta in placental mammals facilitates a longer growth period for the babies in the womb. Marsupials also have an underdeveloped placenta that limits their gestation period.

Anemones

Sea anemones are a group of water-dwelling predatory animals. They are close relatives of corals and jellyfish. They have a cylindrical body with several tentacles surrounding the mouth. They eat small fish and shrimp. They attach themselves to rocks or sea bottoms to escape enemies. They depend upon algae for oxygen and sugar. They do have no specialized sense organs and lack a skeleton. They are poisonous creatures. The poison is a mix of toxins. The poison is used to paralyse the prey.

What are sponges scientifically called?

Sponges

Sea sponges are the simplest multi-cellular animals. They look plant-like. They are quite colourful and beautiful. It is a bottom-dwelling creature which attaches itself to something where it can receive enough food to grow. Their scientific name is Porifera which means pore-bearing. Sea sponges have tiny pores all over their body. Water brings in nutrients and oxygen, and carries out waste and carbon dioxide. Sponges are "filter feeders". They are able to capture and eat even tiny bacteria. Their skeleton is made of tiny needle-like splinters called "spicules". Many sponges are microscopic. Male and female parts are in the same sponge. They produce large amounts of toxins to protect themselves from predators.

Facts

- A sponge can reconstruct itself if it breaks into two.
- Sea anemones inflate themselves to let tides and currents take them to a new location.

Snails, Clams and Oysters

Snails, clams and oysters belong to the family of marine mollusks. Mollusc means soft-bodied. Mollusks have no internal skeleton. They have many shells which act as an external protection. Mollusks are of two types – univalve and bivalve. Univalve mollusks have shell in one piece. Bivalve mollusks have shells in two parts which is connected by a hinge.

Snails

Sea snails are a very large group of animals. Snails living in saltwater breathe using gills. Some even have lungs. Their shells are spirally coiled. Some even have conical shells. Some snails are herbivores and some are omnivores. They use their foot to travel. The foot is a muscular organ spread under the body. They even have tentacles. Their eyes are at the base of their tentacles.

Facts
- Snails do not have teeth and some don't even have eyes.
- Nudibranchs are mollusks without shells.

What does mantle help in?

Clams

The shell of clams is bivalved. They have no head, eyes, teeth, arms or legs. They have kidneys, a heart and a mouth. Clams feed on plankton and are filter feeders. They breathe through gills. Their foot is towards the front of the body.

Oysters

Oysters are bivalved mollusks. Oyster shells are usually oval or pear-shaped. They have a three-chambered heart, colourless blood and two kidneys. They are found on coral reefs and rocks. They breathe through the gills or mantle. Oysters feed on plankton and are filter feeders.

Sea Stars

Sea stars also known as starfish are among the most familiar marine invertebrates. They are spiny, hard-skinned animals. They live on the rocky sea floor. They are found in a wide variety of shapes and sizes. Red stars, fragile stars and blood stars are types of starfish.

Organs and senses

Most of the vital organs like the eyes and nervous system of a starfish are in their arms. They do not have a brain but a complex nervous system which acts like a brain. Nerve rings surround the mouth and run through the entire length of their arms. The most interesting thing about starfish is the manner in which they eat. They are carnivores with their mouth on the underside of the body. Despite this shortcoming, their favourite food is clam, fish and oyster. They climb on top of their prey and lock it with their arms. Then they push their stomach out through their mouth and suck the prey inside when it is nearly digested.

Sea stars have tiny dots on their body called _____ ?

Physical traits

Most sea stars have five arms but cannot swim. They have a spiky shell to protect them. Starfish have hundreds of tiny projections known as tube feet under their body which helps in locomotion. Males and females are not distinguishable from the outside. They have tiny dots called papillae on their entire body. Papillae and tube feet help in respiration.

Facts

- Starfish have the ability to regrow their arms if they are accidentally cut.
- Starfish do not have blood. They have a water vascular system.

Jellyfish

Jellyfish also known as sea jellies are fish-eating animals. They float on the surface as well as deep seas. A few species live in freshwater. They have soft bodies and long, poisonous tentacles. They use their tentacles to catch fish. They have stinging cells in their tentacles which kills their prey. They feed on fish, crustaceans and zooplankton. The most dangerous jellyfish are Australian box jellyfish and Irukandji jellyfish.

Senses and organs

Jellyfish do not have any specialised digestive, respiratory or nervous system. Their skin is very thin which enables them to live without a respiratory system. Their body is oxygenated through diffusion. They lack a brain or central nervous system and have limited control over their movement. They have a loose network of nerves called "nerve net" which they use for sensing other animals. Some have light-sensitive organs that are not able to form images but detect light.

How are jellyfish oxygenated?

Overpopulation

The population of jellyfish has increased over the years. This is because overfishing has reduced the number of jellyfish that eat fish. They even cause harm to swimmers. Sometimes they poison the fish caught in nets that reach humans and lead to the death of the consumer. They eat young fish and fish eggs, which hinders the growth of the fish population. If this pattern continues, jellyfish can lead to the extinction of the animals they feed on.

Facts

- Jellyfish is 98% water.
- The largest jellyfish is the Lion's mane.

Crustaceans

Crustaceans are among the largest group of animals on Earth. This group includes crabs, lobsters, shrimp and krill. The name crustacean comes from a hard and crusty body. Most of them are free-swimming marine organisms. Marine crustaceans feed upon zooplankton and dead organisms for food. They are found in saltwater, freshwater and brackish water all over the world. Some crustaceans are terrestrial while some live as parasites on animals.

Physical make-up

Crustaceans are made up of numerous segments- the head, the thorax and the abdomen. All of these body segments are covered by a hard external shell - exoskeleton. The head has antennae which are a part of the sensory system. Nearly all crustaceans have two eyes which detect light or dark and movement. They have no teeth but their stomachs have teeth to grind and break the food. The food is digested by digestive juices produced in the liver. They breathe through gills and absorb oxygen from the water. The heart is in the abdomen and pumps blood to the entire body. The blood also transports oxygen and food nutrients to cells.

Moulting

A crustacean grows but its exoskeleton does not. The animal must moult its old exoskeleton to adjust its growing body. In moulting the tissue layer under the exoskeleton detaches and secretes a new exoskeleton. When the new skeleton is completely formed, the older one splits along the weak points and the animal expands itself.

Facts

- Crustaceans moult throughout their lives but the frequency decreases with age.
- Each segment of a crustaceans body has a separate pair of legs.

What is the hard outer covering on crustaceans body called?

Eels

Eels are fish but they look like snakes. Unlike other fish, eels do not have scales on their body. Instead, their body is covered with a layer of mucus. The mucus layering makes eels slimy and slippery. They usually live in the deep sea zones and slither between rocks and crevices. Eels are found both in marine water and freshwater around the world. They usually feed on small fish, crustaceans, insects, worms and mollusks.

Freshwater eels

Freshwater eels have a large pointed head and long fins that run from the middle of their back to the tail. This fish is eaten as a delicacy in many parts of Europe. American eel, European eel and Japanese eel are some of the freshwater eels.

Facts

- There are about 600 species of eels and are grouped into 22 families.
- Duckbill eels are also known as witch eels as they have a long narrow snout and sharp tapering tail.

Moray eels

Moray eels are one of the largest species of eels. There are about 200 species of moray eels living in the world oceans. Giant moray eel is the largest and grows to be ten feet long and weighs about 80 pounds. Ribbon eel and spotted moray eel are two of the most amazing looking eels.

Green moray eels

Green moray eels are one of the largest moray eels. They can grow up to eight feet long and weigh up to 65 pounds. Green moray eels are actually brown in colour but they are covered with a thick layer of yellow mucus which makes them appear green. They are found in the Gulf of Mexico, Caribbean Sea and the western Atlantic Ocean.

What is the other name for duckbill eels?

Whales

Whales are large, intelligent aquatic animals that breathe through their lungs. Whales have a sleek and streamlined body that enables them to move easily through the water. They are the only mammals that live their entire lives in the water. Adult whales have no hair on them. Mysticetes (baleen whales) and Odontocetes (toothed whales) are the two types of whales. The most commonly found whales are Southern Right whales, humpback whales and orcas (killer whales).

How do whales eat?

The toothed whales feed on fish and squid. They do not use their teeth to chew but only to capture and tear their food. The baleen whales do not have teeth but baleen: a row of plates that hang like a curtain from both sides of the upper jaw. Baleen plates help in separating water from food. Baleen whales feed on plankton or small fish. Whales allow water to enter their mouths and drain out again with their mouths open.

Do whales use their teeth to chew? (Yes/No)

Threats to whales

A large number of whales are dying due to a number of reasons including contamination in seawater, getting caught in fishing gear and whaling. Before the widespread use of petroleum and plastic, whales provided very valuable raw materials for objects of daily use. Soon, with the discovery of petroleum whaling ceased as petroleum is a cheaper source of oil, but the damage was already done.

Facts
- The life span of a whale is similar to that of a human.
- Blue whale is the largest mammal on earth.

Dolphins and Porpoises

Dolphins and porpoises are marine mammals closely related to whales. Whales, dolphins and porpoises belong to the order *cetacea*. A group of cetaceans is called a pod. Dolphins and porpoises are found worldwide, mostly in the shallower seas of continents. They are carnivores feeding mainly on fish and squid.

Physical traits

Dolphins and porpoises share many similarities when it comes to physical characteristics. Both have streamlined and smooth bodies. Unlike most mammals, cetaceans are hairless. They may have few hair which go away shortly after birth. They breathe through blowholes which are connected to the lungs. There can be one or two blowholes, depending on the species. Some even have a single slit on top of the head. Cetaceans have no external ears and communicate with each other using whistles, clicks and vocalizations. They even make ultrasonic sounds for echolocation.

Differences between dolphins and porpoises

When you first look at a dolphin and a porpoise, both might look very similar. You may not be able to spot the difference between the two. If you look closely both are quite different from each other in some aspects. The first thing that comes to mind when we talk about dolphins is their playful nature. Dolphins not only play among themselves but also with humans. Porpoises are shy and not very playful. If we talk about physical traits, dolphins have a sleek body whereas porpoises are chubbier. Secondly, porpoises do not have a beak but dolphins have a large and prominent beak. Thirdly, dolphins have cone-shaped teeth whereas porpoises have spade-shaped teeth.

Facts
- Cetaceans have no or weak sense of smell.
- Cetaceans have no sweat glands.

Through what do dolphins and porpoises breathe?

Dugongs and Manatees

Manatees and dugongs are huge but gentle animals. They spend their whole lives in water. Since they are mammals they need air to breathe just like us. They come to the surface to breathe. They have flattened tails that help them to swim easily in the water despite their bulky bodies. They rest by floating near the surface or lying at the bottom.

Dugong

Dugongs are large grey mammals. They have nostrils on top of their head. They use their tail and flippers to swim. Their tail is shaped like that of a shark. The only hair they have are the bristles near the mouth. They breathe through their lungs which are long enough to extend to their kidney. They come to the surface to breathe but never come to land. They move very slowly due to their heavy bodies and have little protection from predators. Sharks, saltwater crocodiles and killer whales are a danger to them. They have very small eyes and limited vision with the ears located on the sides of the head. The body structure is the same in males and females.

Where are manatees found?

Manatee

Manatees are large, fully aquatic herbivorous animals. They are found in the shallow waters of the Caribbean Sea and the Gulf of Mexico, floating with the help of their paddle-shaped tail. They have a flexible upper lip used for gathering food and eating. At times they also use the upper lip for communication. Their snout is smaller than that of a dugong. They have small widely – spaced eyes and the eyelids close in a circular manner. Adult manatees do not have canines.

Facts

- The ears of dugongs do not have a pinna.
- Manatees' teeth are replaced continuously throughout life.

Pinnipeds

The word pinniped means fin or flipper-footed. Pinnipeds are marine mammals that have front and rear flippers which help them in moving faster in water. They live in water but are able to come on land for long periods of time. Three commonly found families of pinnipeds are: seals, sea lions and walruses.

Seals

Seals are fish-eating aquatic mammals that have streamlined and sleek bodies. Seals travel in the Atlantic and Pacific Ocean feeding on fish, squid, crustaceans and mussels. They can easily track the movement of nearby objects as they have very good eyesight and very sensitive whiskers. They have flattened corneas and pupils that can open wide to let in light while swimming. Since they stay in icy cold regions they need something to keep them warm. Fat and fur prove helpful for this purpose as they have a thick layer of both on their bodies. Slits replace nostrils in seals and they have the ability to close them under water.

What do seals have in place of nostrils?

Walrus

Walruses are the largest pinnipeds found in the Arctic and Subarctic areas. They like to live in shallow waters. They have prominent tusks which are elongated canines that help in gathering food. They have a thick skin to protect them from predators. They have an air sac under their throat that helps them to move up and down vertically in the water and while sleeping. They eat shrimps, crabs, worms and even parts of other pinnipeds.

Facts

- Pinnipeds come ashore only once a year.
- Walruses change colour when it starts getting colder.

Monsters of the sea

Sharks are amazing fish older than even dinosaurs. They are found in large water bodies all over the world but do not stay in fresh water. Unlike other fish, sharks do not have bones. Instead, their skeleton is made of cartilage – a tough, flexible tissue. They have streamlined bodies but do not have a swim bladder. Sharks commonly eat bony fishes, mollusks, worms and crustaceans.

Senses and organs

Like other fishes, sharks extract oxygen from the water when it passes over their gills. Most sharks need to swim constantly in order to breathe. They cannot sleep for very long as they tend to sink. Sharks have seven senses which include night vision and sense of smell due to which they can see clearly in the dark. Their body temperature is the same as their environment as sharks are cold-blooded animals. They have a strip of red muscle at the centre of their body that generates heat within the body.

How do sharks breathe?

Threats to sharks

Sharks have superior hunting skills but many shark species are now threatened with extinction. The main threats to sharks are over-fishing and accidental catching. Sharks are in very high demand for their meat, skin and cartilage which is used in several medicines and sold at very high prices. If this trend continues then soon sharks will also become extinct like dinosaurs. Conservation efforts taken by humans are difficult as they are unable to fully understand the behaviour and migration patterns of sharks.

Facts
- Whale Shark is the largest fish
- Sharks reproduce either by giving birth to young ones or laying eggs.

Shark fins

Marine Reptiles

Marine reptiles are a group of large and carnivorous animals adapted to staying in water. Marine crocodiles, turtles and sea snakes are the only members of this group alive today.

Sea snakes

Sea snakes are descendants of lizards with 50 species of living in the marine environment. Their body is streamlined and scales are reduced or absent so they can stay in the water. The tail is compressed and is used as a paddle. Most have venomous fangs but they rarely bite humans.

Marine Iguanas

It is the only sea lizard and is found only on Galapagos Islands. Although marine iguanas are fierce-looking lizards yet they are herbivores feeding only on algae and seaweed. They are very good swimmers and have long, sharp claws. They lay eggs in a nest.

Do sea snakes harm humans? (Yes/No)

Marine turtles

Marine turtles are found worldwide and are larger than their land relatives. Most of the species are found in Australian waters. They have a compressed streamlined shell called a 'carapace' and cannot draw their head completely into it. They have four strong paddle-like flippers and like all reptiles use their lungs to breathe.

Facts

- Sea turtles possess a salt excretory gland at the corner of the eye, in the nostrils, or tongue
- Sea snakes have only one lung and it is long enough to reach up to their tail.

Coral Reefs

Coral reefs are living structures made by tiny animals called coral polyps. Many marine plants and animals stay in coral reefs. They are often mistaken for rocks or plants. They are huge, colourful and beautiful reefs made of calcium carbonate. Most reefs were formed when the latest melting of glaciers made the sea level rise. Coral reefs need sunlight, warm and clear shallow water to survive.

The Great Barrier Reef

It is the largest reef system and is the World's biggest single structure made by living organisms. It is located in the Coral Sea near Australia. It supports many animals, mostly endangered species. Some animals found there are whales, turtles, dolphins and porpoises.

What do polyps look like?

Coral polyps

Corals are carnivorous invertebrates. Corals are close relatives of jellyfish and sea anemones. Corals are found all over the world. The animal portion of the reef is called the polyp. Polyps look like a sack with a mouth. There is a ring of tentacles around the mouth. Coral polyps usually live in groups. Each polyp makes a stone-like skeleton around its body. The bodies of polyps are very delicate and decays when they die. The hard skeleton remains even after death and the skeletons of all the dead ones join together. New polyps grow on top of the dead ones. The process of accumulation of skeletons continues and forms reefs.

Facts

- Great Barrier Reef is protected from destruction by Great Barrier Reef Marine Park.
- The crown-of-thorns fish eats coral polyps.

Octopus and Squid

Octopus and squids belong to the order cephalopods—the most intelligent, mobile and largest of all mollusks. They move by expelling water from a tubular siphon under the head. They have a group of muscular sucker-bearing arms. Cuttlefish and chambered nautilus are close relatives of octopus and squids. Cephalopods are diverse in size and lifestyle. They are also referred to as "brainy" invertebrates.

Squid

Squids are fascinating creatures that can be found in saltwater as well as freshwater bodies. They can survive in a variety of temperatures. All squids are cigar-shaped and have a very large head. They have an extremely soft body with no outer shell to support the body or muscles. They are the fastest swimming invertebrates and eat creatures smaller than them.

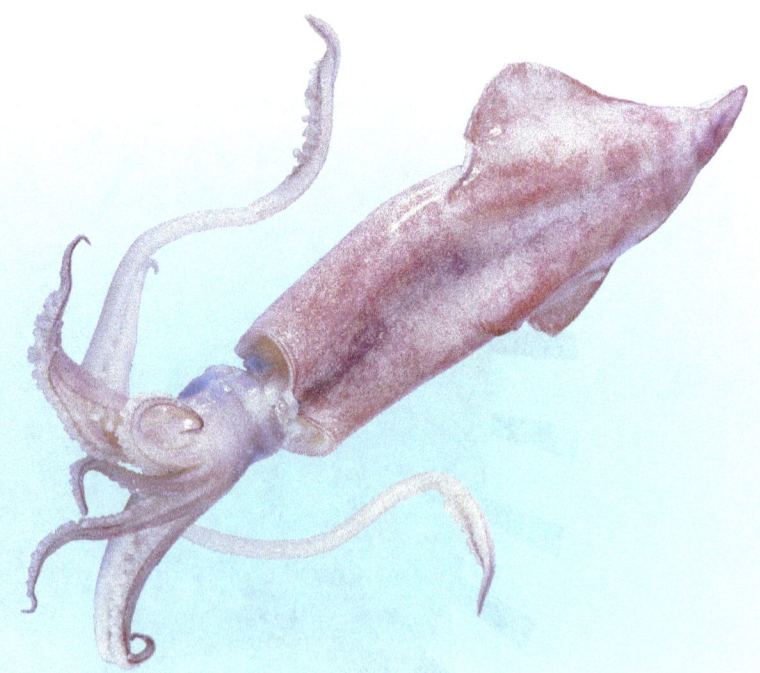

How many arms do octopuses have?

Octopus

Octopuses live in different regions of the sea including the coral reefs. Octopuses have two eyes and four pairs of arms. They have hard beaks and their mouth is located on the underside, where the eight arms meet. Although octopuses have no internal or external skeleton they have three hearts. The lack of skeleton allows them to squeeze through tight places. Octopuses release a cloud of black ink when they sense an enemy. The ink blurs the enemy's vision and also makes the sense of smell weak which gives it time to swim away. If an octopus loses an arm, it can regrow again.

Facts

- The blood of octopuses is blue in colour as it has lots of copper.
- Giant squid and colossal squid are the largest invertebrates in the world.

Extinct Sea Creatures

Extinction is the end of an organism, animal or plant. A species becomes extinct when they are no longer able to survive the changing conditions and the moment of extinction occurs when the last individual of a species dies. The extinction of a large number of species within a relatively short period of time is called mass extinction.

Extinct sea creatures

A number of sea creatures have become extinct over the years. The reasons may be different for different animals. All life forms originated from the sea but all things are subject to change. This change is called evolution. With evolution the environment changes which may be unfavourable for some species. Ichthyosaurus and Labrador duck are some extinct sea creatures.

Facts

- Megalodon was the apex predator of its time was twice as big as the great white shark. Its teeth were as long as 18 centimetres.
- Archelon was a giant sea turtle that lived in the late Cretaceous period about 75 to 65 million years ago.

Ichthyosaurus

The word 'Ichthyosaurus' means lizard fish. The ichthyosaurus was a prehistoric mammal very similar to dolphins. They had the same shape and size as dolphins. They birthed their young ones and swam to the surface for oxygen. Their primary food was fish.

Steller's sea cow

Steller's sea cow was a large herbivorous marine mammal found abundantly throughout North Pacific. Sea cows had no teeth but a horn-like plate in their mouth to chew their food. They depended upon soft food like kelp and seaweed for food. It was a slow-moving animal and got captured easily. They used to float on the sea surface and were easy targets for hunters. These two reasons led to the extinction of the sea cow.

What is the extinction of a large number of species in a short span of time called?

Glossary

Adapt: the ability to change oneself according to the surroundings for survival

Algae: a type of plant with no roots, leaves or steam that grows in water

Canine: pointed or conical teeth

Commercial: related to business or money

Contamination: to make something dirty or polluted

Cornea: a transparent layer that covers the outside of the eyes

Decay: to rot

Echolocation: a technique in which an animal makes a sound which bounces back and returns in the form of echoes which help it in determining its surroundings

Elongate: to become longer

Endangered species: those animals who are on the verge of extinction

Evolution: a gradual change in the growth and development of a living organism

Extinction: an organism that is dead and no longer exists

Gigantic: huge or very large

Hydrophone: an instrument used for detecting sound under water

Invertebrate: an organism without a backbone

Locomotion: the ability to move from one place to another

Migration: a behaviour of travelling to long distances for warmer weather or for breeding

Moult: to lose the outer layer of skin for a new one

Nervous system: an organ system containing a network of cells that coordinate the actions of an animal

Predator: an animal who kills another animal for food

Prehistoric: very old or ancient

Prominent: something which is easy to see or notice

Pupil: the black round part in the middle of the eye

Respiration: the process of breathing in and breathing out air with a pair of lungs

Satellite: an object sent into space to orbit around the earth for receiving and sending information

Seaweed: a plant that grows in the sea

Sediment: a layer of sand, dirt, mud, stone that becomes a layer of rock

Swim bladder: an air bladder inside a fish to keep it afloat

Tentacle: one of the many arms of an animal which it uses for catching prey

Threatened: to be in danger of becoming extinct

Toxin: a poisonous material

Tusk: big teeth jutting out from the mouth of some animals such as elephant, walrus

Vascular system: a system of blood vessels to carry out blood throughout the body

Whaling: the activity of hunting whales

Whisker: long stiff hair that grow near the mouth of some animals

Answers

Page No. 51   Chordates/Mollusks/Arthropods

Page No. 52   Autotrophs

Page No. 55   Ichthyology

Page No. 56   Porifera

Page No. 58   Respiration, shell growth and colour

Page No. 60   Papillae

Page No. 62   Diffusion

Page No. 65   Exoskeleton

Page No. 67   Witch eels

Page No. 68   No

Page No. 71   Blowholes

Page No. 72   Shallow seas of the Caribbean Sea and the Gulf of Mexico

Page No. 74   Slits

Page No. 76   Gills

Page No. 78   No

Page No. 80   Sack with a mouth

Page No. 82   4 pairs (8)

Page No. 85   Mass extinction

www.ingramcontent.com/pod-product-compliance
Lightning Source LLC
Chambersburg PA
CBHW050658160426
43194CB00010B/1986